MANDALAS
COLORING BOOK

MARTY NOBLE
ALBERTA HUTCHINSON

DOVER PUBLICATIONS, INC.
MINEOLA, NEW YORK

Copyright

Copyright © 2007 by Alberta Hutchinson
Copyright © 2012, 2014 by Dover Publications, Inc.
All rights reserved.

Bibliographical Note

Mandalas Coloring Book contains all the plates from the following previously published Dover books: *Nature Mandalas* (designs 1–31) by Marty Noble, and *Mystical Mandalas* (designs 32–63) by Alberta Hutchinson.

International Standard Book Number

ISBN-13: 978-0-486-80352-4
ISBN-10: 0-486-80352-X

Manufactured in the United States by RR Donnelley
80352X06   2016
www.doverpublications.com